Original title:
Whispers Woven in Wonder

Copyright © 2024 Creative Arts Management OÜ
All rights reserved.

Author: Gideon Barrett
ISBN HARDBACK: 978-9916-90-544-9
ISBN PAPERBACK: 978-9916-90-545-6

Threads of Enigma and Grace

In shadows dance the threads of fate,
Woven tight with whispers great,
Mystery cloaked in soft embrace,
A tapestry of time and space.

Glimmers of light through shadows peek,
A silent heart begins to speak,
Journey carved in silken lace,
Each step taken, a sacred trace.

Lost in dreams, the visions twine,
Glimmering hints of the divine,
With every twist, a hidden place,
Where secrets linger, wrapped in grace.

Threads connect the known and naught,
In quiet moments, treasures sought,
The dance of life, a dance of grace,
In the enigma, find your space.

Echoing Through the Canopy

Whispers dance among the leaves,
Soft secrets carried on the breeze.
Shadows play where sunlight weaves,
Nature's song puts hearts at ease.

Branches sway with gentle grace,
Life abounds in this lush space.
Each echo tells a tale of lace,
Binding earth in an embrace.

Birds take flight in vibrant hue,
Fluttering softly, skies so blue.
Their songs resound, both tried and true,
A symphony that feels anew.

In this realm of green and light,
Hope awakens from the night.
Through the canopy's embrace so tight,
Dreams take wing, prepared for flight.

Mysteries Beneath the Surface

Ripples shimmer on the lake,
Depths conceal what dreams forsake.
Secrets linger in the wake,
Whispers of the things we make.

Shadows dwell in water's hold,
Silence speaks of stories told.
Mysteries wrapped in depths so cold,
A world beneath, both brave and bold.

Creatures glide where few have seen,
In the dark, life flows serene.
Hidden realms where what has been,
Lives anew, a cryptic scene.

Glimmers flicker, beckon near,
Illusions fade, yet truths appear.
In the depths, there's naught to fear,
For every wave brings voices clear.

Hints of Dawn's Embrace

Softly glows the morning light,
Whispers fade away from night.
Gentle warmth begins to rise,
Painting colors in the skies.

Birds awake with tender song,
Nature's pulse, a beat so strong.
Hints of dawn where dreams belong,
In this moment, hearts feel wrong.

Golden rays on dewdrops rest,
Nature's beauty at its best.
Each breath taken, pure and blessed,
In the dawn, our souls invest.

As shadows stretch and night moves on,
We greet the day, a brand new dawn.
With open arms, we carry on,
Embracing life, from dusk to dawn.

The Gentle Call of the Unknown

A soft voice calls from distant shores,
It stirs the soul, it gently pours.
Curiosity, an open door,
Inviting hearts to seek for more.

Through the mist, paths intertwine,
Whispers laced in ivy vine.
Every step brings truth divine,
Adventures in the grand design.

Mountains rise, and valleys sway,
Echoes of what lies away.
In each shadow, light will play,
Guiding those who dare to stray.

With every breath, the world will sing,
A tapestry of everything.
The unknown is a wondrous spring,
A gentle call, the heart's offering.

Secrets of the Starlit Veil

Beneath the night, a whisper flows,
Stars blink secrets, no one knows.
Moonlight wraps the world in grace,
Time stands still in this sacred space.

Winds weave tales of ancient lore,
Guiding hearts to an open door.
Each twinkle hides a hidden truth,
Waiting for the touch of youth.

Dreams Danced on a Breeze

Catch the soft sigh of the night,
Where dreams take wing and catch the light.
They twirl and sway like leaves in flight,
Painting the sky with pure delight.

Whispers of hope on gentle winds,
A symphony where longing begins.
In the silence, dreams softly blend,
Carried on breezes, they transcend.

Reflections in the Twilight

Golden hues in twilight's embrace,
Mirrors of moments, time cannot erase.
Shadows linger, thoughts unfurl,
In the stillness, life starts to twirl.

Glances exchanged in fading light,
Fleeting feelings spark the night.
Each heartbeat echoes with the past,
An endless dance, forever cast.

Shadows of a Dreamscape

In the realm where dreams reside,
Shadows dance, and phantoms glide.
Whispers linger, voices call,
In this world, we rise and fall.

Colors blend in twilight's hue,
A surreal landscape, vast and new.
In every corner, mysteries lie,
Woven together, a secret sigh.

Chants of the Barefoot Shadows

In the silent glade where whispers dwell,
  Shadows dance and weave a spell.
    Barefoot echoes on the ground,
      Ghostly secrets all around.

    Moonlit paths of silver light,
Guide the way through mystic night.
    Every step a tale retold,
Barefoot shadows brave and bold.

    Rustling leaves beneath the stars,
   Mark the journey, heal old scars.
    Nature's chorus fills the air,
  Chants of life, of love, of care.

With every dusk, their voices rise,
    Soft and sweet like lullabies.
  In the woods where spirits roam,
Barefoot shadows find their home.

Hushed Songs of the Night

Underneath the velvet sky,
Crickets sing and owls reply.
Stars are dots of ancient light,
Hushed are songs of deepest night.

Shadows waltz on silver streams,
Hushed whispers cradle fragile dreams.
In the stillness, hearts will sway,
Night enfolds the end of day.

A nocturnal serenade,
In the twilight, fears do fade.
Every murmur, soft and low,
Guides lost souls where rivers flow.

With the moon, their voices blend,
Carried forth on winds that bend.
Hushed songs weave the darkened air,
Promised peace, a tender prayer.

Lullabies Among the Leaves

In the canopy so high,
Gentle breezes pass on by.
Lullabies of leaf and tree,
Hold the child close, let them be.

Softly sung in twilight's hue,
Nature's melodies come through.
Rustling leaves, a soothing sound,
Peaceful dreams in green abound.

Cradled in the arms of night,
Stars twinkle with loving light.
Every note, a soft caress,
Woven deep in wilderness.

As the world breathes in and out,
Nature sings, dispelling doubt.
Lullabies will never cease,
In the leaves, a song of peace.

The Tapestry of Time Unraveled

Threads of moments knit with care,
Whispers of the past lay bare.
Each stitch formed with joy or tears,
Woven tales across the years.

In the fabric of the night,
Every shadow holds a light.
Time unravels, tales unfold,
Fables woven, lives retold.

Through the ages, we will weave,
Stories only hearts believe.
Time a river, ever flow,
Carrying us where we go.

With each passing breath we make,
New patterns in the dreams we stake.
The tapestry of life so vast,
Links our futures to the past.

The Unseen Symphony of Life

In silence whispers the heart's refrain,
Notes of joy and echoes of pain.
Each breath a chord, a story to weave,
In the unseen dance, we quietly believe.

The trees sway gently, a graceful tune,
As stars twinkle bright, beneath the moon.
Waves crash softly, a tender embrace,
Life's symphony plays, with delicate grace.

Patterns of the Untangled

Threads of fate in colors entwined,
Stories of old, in silence designed.
Each knot reveals what we thought was lost,
Patterns emerge, regardless of cost.

Fractals of time, in the mind's eye,
Unraveling paths as we learn to fly.
Life's tapestry rich, yet simple and grand,
Reveals in each twist where we choose to stand.

The Soul's Unspoken Journey

In whispered dreams where shadows dwell,
A journey unfurls, too deep to tell.
Each step a secret, each pause a sigh,
Through valleys of silence, under the sky.

Footprints on sand, washed by the tide,
Echoes of longing that won't subside.
The heart seeks a home, where truth can ignite,
In the quiet moments, our souls take flight.

Revelations Beneath the Moonlight

Under moon's glow, truths softly gleam,
Veils of the night dissolve like a dream.
Whispers of wisdom float on the breeze,
As shadows reveal what the heart sees.

Stars are confessions in a celestial rhyme,
Guiding the wanderers lost in time.
The night holds secrets of love and despair,
Bathed in the glow, we lay our souls bare.

Tentative Touches of Fate.

In the whisper of shadows,
Paths cross in the twilight.
Fingers brush like feathers,
Unseen choices take flight.

Moments dance on the edge,
Hearts tremble, a soft sigh.
Destinies weave fine patterns,
As time winks goodbye.

Faint glimmers of what's near,
Guided by a gentle pull.
Steps taken, quietly unsure,
Each heartbeat feels so full.

A glance exchanged in silence,
Two souls know the game played.
In tentative touches of fate,
The future's softly laid.

Silent Threads of Enchantment

In the night's gentle embrace,
Stars twinkle like secrets kept.
Whispers travel through the dark,
In their warmth, dreams are swept.

Threads of silver glisten bright,
Tales of love and hope unite.
Each beat of a hidden heart,
Echoes softly in the night.

With every breath, the magic flows,
In the stillness, shadows speak.
Silent threads of enchantment,
Binding souls that long to seek.

Lost in dreams, we wander free,
Wrapped in night's ethereal sea.
Every moment pulses alive,
In silent threads, we find our key.

Echoes of the Unseen

Through the mist, a soft call rings,
Unseen voices drift and weave.
Like fleeting thoughts on a breeze,
Whispers linger, never leave.

In the emptiness retreat,
Promises float without a date.
Echoes dance beneath the stars,
Shadows twist, their quiet fate.

Time unravels in whispers sweet,
Gentle impact on the heart.
Each echo fades but is not lost,
A tapestry of hope's art.

Feel the pulse of distant dreams,
Awakening with every beat.
In the echoes of the unseen,
We find paths beneath our feet.

Murmurs in the Mist

Veils of gray stretch thin and wide,
Murmurs dance upon the air.
Secrets hidden, softly glide,
In each layer, tales we share.

Nature sings a quiet song,
With the rustle of the leaves.
In the mist, where shadows belong,
The heart whispers, and believes.

Walking paths of memories,
Lost in fog's enchanting maze.
Murmurs rise like fluttering wings,
Catching dreams in gentle sways.

Life unfolds in tender sighs,
Each breath wrapped in soft embrace.
Murmurs in the mist arise,
Carrying hope in their trace.

The Quiet Beneath the Noise

In crowded streets, silence hums,
A whisper lost, where chaos drums.
Between the clamor, stillness grows,
The heart, a quiet place it knows.

Beneath the rush, soft shadows glide,
Moments where hidden dreams confide.
In the raucous, peace takes flight,
A secret found in the fading light.

Echoes of calm in the loudest din,
A gentle breath where life begins.
In every shout a soft refrain,
The quiet calls, like summer rain.

The Hidden Song of Solitude

In stillness blooms a melody,
Notes unplayed, yet wild and free.
The heart composes, soft and low,
A tune that only silence knows.

Alone with thoughts, the spirit sings,
In quietude, the soul takes wing.
Each pause creates a symphony,
The heart's own song, a mystery.

Through whispered winds and twilight skies,
Loneliness wears a sweet disguise.
A chorus found in the night's embrace,
In solitude, we find our space.

Threads of Celestial Stories

Stars weave tales in the velvet night,
Galaxies dance, an endless flight.
Each twinkle holds a whispered sigh,
A tale of ages, drifting by.

In cosmic webs, our fates entwine,
A spark of hope in the grand design.
Infinite worlds, yet here we stand,
Connected threads in a timeless strand.

Dreams are carried on starlit streams,
The universe hums with our hidden dreams.
In the quiet of night, reflections glow,
Unseen paths where the heart may go.

Secrets of the Swaying Willows

Whispers weave through willow trees,
Dancing gently with the breeze.
Secrets held in tangled roots,
A symphony of leafy flutes.

Their branches sway, a graceful dance,
Inviting thoughts, a soft romance.
In shadows deep, lies wisdom's song,
A hidden world where dreams belong.

Beneath their shade, the stories flow,
Of laughter, tears, and love's soft glow.
In each rustle, ancient tales arise,
The willows watch under starlit skies.

Traces of a Timeless Melody

In quiet corners, shadows play,
A song of whispers drifts away.
Notes entwined with fading light,
Echoes linger, soft and bright.

Memories wrapped in warm embrace,
Dance to rhythms time won't chase.
Each heartbeat hums a gentle tune,
Underneath the watchful moon.

Strings of fate pull memories near,
Melodies that only we hear.
In the silence, hope unfurls,
A symphony of unknown worlds.

Through the silence, notes still glide,
Carrying dreams where secrets hide.
In the air, an old refrain,
Calls us back to love again.

The Play of Light on Water

Sunlight dances on the sea,
Waves reflecting harmony.
Rippling colors, bright and clear,
Nature's canvas, year to year.

Gentle whispers, breezes sigh,
Shimmering dreams as they fly by.
In this moment, time stands still,
Water's magic, heart's great thrill.

Clouds like shadows, drifting slow,
Painting scenes, a tranquil glow.
Every movement tells a tale,
A fleeting breath, a soft exhale.

Harmony of light and tide,
All of nature's joy and pride.
The world in ripples, vast and wide,
In this dance, we all abide.

Unseen Threads of Connection

In the tapestry of time we weave,
Invisible threads that we believe.
Connections made with silent grace,
Knit our hearts in every space.

Through laughter shared and tears we shed,
Every word, a path we tread.
Bridges built without a sight,
Binding souls in love's pure light.

In crowded rooms, we find our way,
Crossing paths at close of day.
With every glance and every smile,
We share a bond that stretches miles.

Around us flows a gentle stream,
Of unspoken bonds and shared dream.
Though unseen, they hold us tight,
In life's great dance, they shine so bright.

Whispers in the Garden of Dreams

In the garden where dreams reside,
Petals whisper secrets, side by side.
Each flower holds a story true,
In colors vibrant, fresh as dew.

Breezes carry tales untold,
Of wishes new and charms of old.
Through fragrant blooms, our hopes align,
In this enclave, hearts intertwine.

Evenings glow with twilight's brush,
As stars awaken, spark a hush.
In the quiet, dreams will spin,
As moonlit shadows softly grin.

Among the leaves, we find our peace,
A sanctuary where fears cease.
In the whispers of the night,
We gather strength and take our flight.

Reverberations of a Fabled Past

Whispers of ages, lost and found,
Tales of glory in the ground.
In shadows cast, the truth does dwell,
Echoes of yore, they weave and swell.

Faded glories, a tapestry spun,
Threads of history, one by one.
Legends linger, in twilight's hue,
Awakened dreams, in morning dew.

Voices of ancients, calling near,
In every heartbeat, they appear.
Memories linger, like smoke in air,
Reverberations, soft yet fair.

In every corner, stories lie,
Waiting for whispers, to soar and fly.
The past, a mirror, reflecting bright,
Guiding us gently, through the night.

Dances of Distant Echoes

Underneath the starry skies,
Footsteps linger, spirit flies.
In the moonlight's tender glow,
Dances swirl and gently flow.

Time's embrace, a fleeting chance,
Echoes tease, a silent dance.
Whirling shadows, lost in dream,
In the night, their voices gleam.

Softly spoken, songs of old,
Creating warmth when nights are cold.
Echoes whisper, tales to share,
Each note a secret, laid bare.

Memories twirl, like leaves in fall,
Shapes and forms, they rise and call.
In this moment, hearts take flight,
Dances cherished, out of sight.

The Enigma of the Softest Sound

A murmur fades into the night,
Quiet secrets take to flight.
Every whisper holds a key,
Unlocking dreams that long to be.

In the stillness, feelings bloom,
Softest sound dispels the gloom.
Hearts entwined in hushed embrace,
In silence found, a sacred space.

Gentle breezes, voices sigh,
Echoes linger, drifting by.
In soft colors, emotions blend,
Mysteries unfold, hearts mend.

The sound of love, a tender tune,
Carried softly, beneath the moon.
An enigma, cherished and profound,
In the quiet, love is found.

Hidden Pathways of the Heart

Winding trails, the heart does seek,
Paths untraveled, voices speak.
In the silence, secrets dwell,
Stories waiting, to be told well.

Amidst the thorns, blossoms grow,
Tender feelings, soft and slow.
Every turn hides a surprise,
In hidden paths, love never lies.

Underneath the twilight's gaze,
Shadows dance in gentle haze.
Every heartbeat, a guiding light,
Leading us through the heart's night.

In each corner, a beacon glows,
Unseen journeys, love bestows.
Pathways hidden, yet so near,
In every step, our dreams appear.

Unseen Forces of Fate

In whispers low, the winds do sway,
They carry dreams, then drift away.
Twisting paths where shadows roam,
Unseen hands guide us home.

With every choice, a ripple spins,
A tale begins, where time thins.
Stars above in silent grace,
Mark the steps, the sacred space.

We are but threads in fate's design,
Woven close, yet hard to find.
Each heartbeat, every glance,
A fated dance, a fleeting chance.

In the dark, hope softly glows,
Through unseen forces, courage grows.
Embrace the mystery, take that leap,
For in the depths, the soul will keep.

Intricacies of the Ethereal

Behind the veil, where spirits play,
Ethereal dreams drift and sway.
Colors blend in spectral light,
A world unfurls within the night.

Threads of silver, whispers clear,
Connect the realms that we hold dear.
In every sigh, a secret gleams,
We dance through life, entwined in dreams.

Mysteries weave a subtle thread,
Guiding us where fears are shed.
In every heartbeat, echoes call,
The force that binds enwraps us all.

Together we explore the skies,
With open hearts, we learn to rise.
In this realm, with love, we soar,
Embracing all that's yet in store.

Veils of Enchantment

In twilight's hush, enchantments blend,
Illusions linger, dreams transcend.
Beneath the moon's soft, glowing hue,
Veils of magic weave anew.

A flicker here, a shimmer there,
Mystic whispers fill the air.
Forest paths, a hidden lore,
Lead to wonders to explore.

Stars above, like watches bright,
Guard our secrets through the night.
In shadows cast, we dare to seek,
A heartbeat's pulse, the magic's peak.

Through ancient woods, the echoes flow,
In gentle sighs, the secrets grow.
Rejoice in spells that twine and twirl,
For charm resides in every swirl.

The Language of Shadows

In silent corners, shadows creep,
Tales untold in whispers seep.
They dance with light, a fleeting grace,
Sketching dreams in empty space.

With every flicker, stories form,
A world reborn, both strange and warm.
Emotions painted, dark and bright,
The language speaks in blurred twilight.

Each silhouette, a fleeting guide,
Reveals the truths that we can't hide.
In echo's breath, they softly roam,
A place where souls can find their home.

Unraveling threads, we come to learn,
The shadows teach what hearts discern.
In every glance, a tale unfolds,
In the language of shadows, life beholds.

Songs from the Starlit Veil

Whispers of night softly call,
Melodies bright, they rise and fall.
Under a sky where stars entwine,
Each note a glimmer, a spark divine.

Winds carry tales from afar,
Echoing brightly, a guiding star.
Hearts attune to the cosmic song,
In this dance, we all belong.

Lost in dreams where shadows play,
Magic awakes at the break of day.
With every chord, our spirits soar,
In the starlit veil, forever more.

Laughter and silence take their place,
In a symphony written in space.
A tapestry woven with light so frail,
Together we sing from the starlit veil.

Hushed Dreams in Harmony

In the quiet of twilight's embrace,
Hushed whispers weave a gentle grace.
Moonlight spills on secrets deep,
In this moment, our dreams take leap.

Hearts beat softly, a rhythmic sound,
In harmony where magic is found.
Each sigh a promise, a wish unspoken,
In the night's still air, a bond unbroken.

Stars align in a dance sublime,
Time stands still, a sacred rhyme.
Cradled in peace, our voices blend,
Hushed dreams unfolding, a timeless trend.

Together we soar on whispers of night,
In a symphony bathed in silver light.
With every heartbeat, our souls ignite,
In this harmony, all feels right.

Breeze of the Hidden Realm

Where whispers linger, and shadows stir,
A breeze dances 'round, soft as a fur.
It carries tales from lands unknown,
Through hidden paths, its secrets are sown.

Glimmers of sunlight filter through trees,
As nature hums with forgotten ease.
Each touch of wind, a gentle caress,
In the hidden realm, we find our rest.

Echoes of laughter drift in the air,
With every rustle, a promise to share.
In the realms where magic still thrives,
The breeze whispers softly, where wonder arrives.

Awakening senses with each allured sigh,
In the dance of the leaves, we learn to fly.
The breeze of the hidden realm calls us near,
In its embrace, we stand without fear.

Shadows of Celestial Curiosity

In the twilight where shadows lay,
Curiosity stirs, come what may.
Stars twinkle down with knowing eyes,
Inviting us to explore the skies.

With each step, the universe unfolds,
Mysteries hidden, as history molds.
Questions linger in the evening's glow,
In shadows deep, new paths we'll sow.

Galaxies whisper in forgotten tongues,
Tales of the old, where the new belongs.
Beneath the veil of the night's embrace,
We chase the echoes of timeless grace.

In every shadow where wonder thrives,
Celestial curiosity breathes and strives.
Together we wander where dreams ignite,
In shadows deep, we glimpse the light.

Whispers Between the Stars

In the night, the silence hums,
Softly with the dreams that come.
Stars above, they twinkle bright,
Sending whispers, pure delight.

Gentle winds caress the night,
Guiding thoughts to take their flight.
In this space where shadows blend,
Whispers linger, never end.

Moonlit paths of silver gleam,
Woven into every dream.
Tell me tales of things unseen,
In the dark, they intervene.

Hope ignites in jeweled skies,
As we dance with cosmic cries.
Every flash a word, a thought,
Within the stars, the truth is sought.

Echoing Secrets of the Soul

Within the depths, a voice does call,
Whispers echo, never fall.
In the heart where shadows play,
Secrets weave in night and day.

Memories drift through silent streams,
Carving paths of broken dreams.
Every echo holds a key,
Unlocking what's meant to be.

In the stillness, truths will rise,
Glimpses caught in secret eyes.
What the heart dares to conceal,
In these echoes, we can feel.

Journey deep where silence reigns,
Cascading through unfed pains.
In the whispers, we are whole,
Finding peace within the soul.

Lurking Truths in a Dreamscape

In the haze where shadows twine,
Lurking truths in every line.
Dreams unfold like fragile light,
Guiding souls through endless night.

Figures dance in moonlit gleam,
Whispers linger, soft as cream.
What is real, what is not?
In the dreamscape, time forgot.

Hidden paths in twilight's gaze,
Lead us through a mystic maze.
Every turn, a chance to find,
Fragments of a woven mind.

In this realm where visions play,
Truths emerge and fade away.
Lost in dreams, yet still we seek,
Answers in the silence speak.

Melodies Hidden in Silence

In the quiet, tunes ascend,
Softly whispered, time to mend.
Beyond the noise, the heart can hear,
Melodies that draw us near.

Gentle strings of fate entwine,
Crafting songs from love's design.
In the silence, music swells,
Echoes weave their secret spells.

Every note a story told,
Vibes of warmth in strands of gold.
From the stillness, life takes flight,
Bringing joy through darkest night.

Swaying softly, lost in grace,
Harmony finds its rightful place.
In the hush where hearts align,
Melodies remain divine.

Caresses of the Moonlight

In night's embrace, she softly glows,
Whispers of dreams in silent throes.
Her silver touch on shadows play,
Guiding hearts that lost their way.

Breezes carry her tender sighs,
Stirring the soul where magic lies.
Each flicker of light, a gentle kiss,
In moonlit dance, we find our bliss.

Subtle Serenades of the Cosmos

Stars align in velvet skies,
Their melodies, a sweet surprise.
Echoes of ancient tales of old,
Sung in harmonies, bright and bold.

Galaxies twirl in cosmic grace,
Whispers of love from space to space.
Each note weaves through the night so deep,
Awakening dreams buried in sleep.

Glimmers of the Forgotten

Flickers of time in shadows cast,
Memories fade but echoes last.
Lost in the mists of yesteryear,
Whispers beckoning, soft and clear.

Treasures hidden in the sands,
Stories told by ancient hands.
With each glimmer, we seek to find,
The remnants of the ties that bind.

Soft Calls of the Enchanted

In the forest, where magic stirs,
Songs of the fairies, like gentle purrs.
Leaves murmur secrets, soft and sweet,
Nature's breath beneath our feet.

Moonbeams dance on the river's flow,
Inviting us where the wild things grow.
In every heartbeat, a story lives,
As soft calls linger, the heart forgives.

Beneath the Surface of Silence

Whispers linger in the air,
Secrets buried everywhere.
In the stillness, hearts can hear,
A symphony that draws us near.

Ripples dance upon the pond,
Beckoning dreams to venture beyond.
In the quiet, truths unfold,
Stories waiting to be told.

Silent shadows weave and sway,
Guiding souls who've lost their way.
Beneath the calm, a pulse ignites,
Fueling hopes and soft delights.

Echoes murmur through the night,
Carrying whispers pure and bright.
In the depths of gentle breath,
Lies the dance of life and death.

The Labyrinth of Lost Echoes

In the maze where shadows dwell,
Each twist and turn, a fleeting spell.
Footsteps fade on cobblestone,
Voices linger, but alone.

Mirrors flash with ghostly grace,
Reflections hide in every place.
Chasing echoes of the past,
Fractured memories that hold fast.

Candles flicker, drawing breath,
Illuminating thoughts of death.
Paths diverge, the heart must choose,
In this maze, we may lose.

Yet through the dark, a light will gleam,
Hope persists beyond the dream.
Lost but seeking, we are brave,
In the labyrinth, we are saved.

A Dappled Path of Imagination

Beneath the boughs of emerald leaves,
A wandering heart, the soul believes.
Sunlight dances on the ground,
In this realm, new worlds abound.

Footfalls trace the shades on grass,
Every step a moment passed.
Whispers swirl in fragrant air,
Tales of wonder everywhere.

Glimmers spark in twilight's glow,
In this place, our minds will flow.
With every sigh, the myths ignite,
Guided by the stars at night.

Together we weave dreams so fine,
Magic lives in every line.
On this path, forever roam,
For imagination finds its home.

The Candor of Shadows

In the dusk, shadows softly rise,
Truths revealed in disguise.
Testing hearts with gentle hands,
Promises made, like shifting sands.

Their embrace, both sweet and cold,
A dance of secrets, brave and bold.
Whispers float like autumn leaves,
Caught between what one believes.

In their depths, we find our fears,
Yet laughter mingles with our tears.
Candor wrapped in twilight's cloth,
Holding tight to what we swore.

So, in the dark, we take a stand,
Trusting shadows, hand in hand.
For in their depth, we learn to see,
The beauty born from honesty.

Silhouettes at Dusk

Shadows stretch across the ground,
As the day begins to fade.
Whispers in the cooling air,
Nature's symphony played.

Figures dance in twilight's glow,
Silhouettes against the sun.
In the hush, the world slows down,
As daylight's battle's won.

Colors blend in fading light,
Crickets start their serenade.
Echoes of a past delight,
In dusk's embrace, they wade.

The horizon swallows the beam,
Night unfurls its silken shroud.
In this hour, we start to dream,
Amongst the gathering crowd.

The Canvas of Night's Secrets

In the dark, the stars ignite,
Each a spark of ancient lore.
Whispered tales of silent night,
Painting dreams we can't ignore.

Moonlight spills like liquid silver,
On landscapes steeped in mystery.
A gentle brush of night's quiver,
Where shadows hold their history.

Breezes carry secrets old,
Through the trees, they softly sigh.
Every rustle, every fold,
Breathes the stories woven high.

In this realm of hushed delight,
Magic dances, dreams entwine.
The canvas speaks without a fight,
In the stillness, all is fine.

The Faint Breath of Daydreams

In the morning's tender light,
Daydreams linger, soft and sweet.
Thoughts like petals take to flight,
With the sun, their hearts do beat.

Whispers of a carefree mind,
Wandering through meadows wide.
In a realm where dreams unwind,
Time and space cannot divide.

Every sigh a wish unspooled,
Dancing like the butterflies.
In this world, the heart is fooled,
As wonder paints the skies.

Faint and fleeting, yet so bright,
These daydreams cradle hopes anew.
In the warmth of dawn's delight,
A canvas for the soul's view.

The Nest of Ancient Memories

In quiet corners, shadows creep,
Nestled where the old tales dwell.
Whispers linger, secrets keep,
In the echoes, stories swell.

Time has stitched a patchwork quilt,
Memories like fragile thread.
Every fold, a heart's soft tilt,
In the warmth of things unsaid.

Photographs of laughter shared,
Faded smiles in sepia hue.
In this nest, love was declared,
Fragments of a life we knew.

The past is woven, rich and deep,
With every thread, a tale unfolds.
In the heart, the echoes seep,
A treasure chest of memories holds.

Celestial Whimsy in the Air

In the stillness of the night,
Whispers of the cosmos play,
Nebulas twirl with delight,
Dancing lights bloom and sway.

Dreams ride on luminous beams,
As the moon's soft glow embraces,
Magic weaves through waking dreams,
Painting smiles on hidden faces.

Stars converse in silent glees,
Every twinkle, a sweet song,
Gentle breezes stir the leaves,
Nature hums where hearts belong.

So let go of earthly cares,
Breathe the wonder in the air,
Among celestial affairs,
We find solace everywhere.

The Hidden Dance of the Stars

In velvet nights, they come alive,
A ballet spun in cosmic grace,
Each star a dancer, free to thrive,
In an endless, boundless space.

The constellations weave a tale,
Of love and loss, of hope and fear,
Their light a ship, in time we sail,
With dreams of all we hold so dear.

Shadows whisper, secrets call,
In the dark, the heart will see,
How each twinkle, large or small,
Marks the steps of destiny.

As they waltz through endless night,
The universe holds its breath,
In the silence, we find light,
In their dance, we conquer death.

Tender Threads of Fate

Upon the loom of life we tread,
Each choice a thread, each moment spun,
In colors bold, in shades of red,
The tapestry of fate begun.

The weaver's hands are gentle, sure,
Guiding paths through joy and strife,
In every knot, a story pure,
Stitched with love, the fabric of life.

With tender care, the strands connect,
Binding hearts through joy and pain,
Each twist a lesson to reflect,
In sunshine's glow, and gentle rain.

So heed the threads, their subtle signs,
For in their weave, the heart finds peace,
Through every choice, love reassures,
In this grand design, our souls release.

Echoes in the Quietude

In the hush of early dawn,
Whispers dance on morning's breath,
Nature's song is softly drawn,
In the stillness, life finds depth.

Echoes linger in the trees,
Carried on the cool wind's sigh,
Memories flow with gentle ease,
In silence, dreams begin to fly.

The heartbeats pulse in tender waves,
As time stretches, slow and sweet,
In quietude, the spirit braves,
Finding peace where stillness meets.

So cherish moments, soft and rare,
For in the calm, our truths appear,
In echoes of the love we share,
We find our way, with hearts sincere.

The Lull of Secrets

In whispers soft, the night unfurls,
Cradling dreams in its velvet twirls.
Secrets hidden, soft and deep,
Wrapped in shadows, they gently sleep.

Stars above, like watchful eyes,
Guard the tales of silent sighs.
Memories linger, softly spun,
In the stillness, all is one.

The breeze carries an old refrain,
Songs of joy, and hints of pain.
As time slips past in gentle grace,
Each heartbeat finds its rightful place.

With dawn's light, the whispers fade,
Yet in our hearts, the echoes played.
In every sigh, a secret kept,
In the lull of night, we softly slept.

The Dance of Forgotten Echoes

In halls of time, where shadows glide,
Forgotten tales in silence bide.
Echoes gather in fleeting forms,
Whirling softly in ghostly swarms.

The music fades yet lingers near,
A haunting tune, both sweet and clear.
Footsteps trace the paths once bold,
In memories, the stories told.

With every turn, the past awakes,
In the dreamscape, where silence shakes.
Dancers swirl in spectral light,
Chasing whispers through the night.

Yet as dawn begins to break,
The echoes fade, illusions shake.
In our hearts, they leave a mark,
The dance of dusk, the dawn's spark.

In the Embrace of the Enchanted

In forests deep, where magic stirs,
The air is thick with whispered purrs.
Each leaf a tale, each root a song,
In the embrace, we all belong.

Moonlight bathes the silent glade,
Where dreams are woven, softly laid.
The night unfolds its mystic thread,
In this place, where fears are shed.

Creatures flit in shadows cast,
Beneath the stars, so vast, so fast.
They dance with grace, both wild and free,
In the realm of fantasy.

With every heartbeat, magic swells,
In the stories that the forest tells.
Lost in wonder, time stands still,
In the embrace of the enchanted will.

Specters of Serenity

In twilight hues, the spirits roam,
Whispers of peace call us home.
Softly they glide on the evening breeze,
Filling the air with gentle ease.

Each sigh of wind, a tender grace,
Serenity finds its rightful place.
Within the still, the world holds breath,
Celebrating life amidst sweet death.

Holding time in a warm embrace,
They gather 'round, in time and space.
Visions of calm in shadows blend,
Where every moment starts to mend.

As night descends, the specters sing,
Of love and hope, of blossomed spring.
In their lullabies, we are set free,
Amidst the whispers of serenity.

Whirls of Unseen Energy

In shadows dance the whispers,
Of currents felt but never seen.
They weave through time like ribbons,
Binding realms, a hidden sheen.

Flickers in the silent night,
Sparkling dreams in cosmic flow.
Each pulse a spark of magic,
In the dark where secrets glow.

Momentum spins the heartbeats,
In harmony they glide and weep.
The fabric of the universe,
Awakens where the dormant sleep.

Caught within this vibrant surge,
Life's rhythm hums, an endless tide.
Embrace the whirls of unseen force,
Let the energy be your guide.

Fleeting Glances of Eternity

In moments brief, the world aligns,
A fleeting breath, a spark ignites.
Time stretches, bends, then softly fades,
In glances shared, the heart knows light.

With every tick, the cosmos spins,
Yet love endures, a timeless dance.
In echoes of a whispered past,
We find ourselves in fleeting chance.

Eternity held in a blink,
Memory's whisper, soft and clear.
We taste the sweetness yet to come,
As moments fade, we hold them dear.

Each glance a thread within the weave,
Of all that's lived, and all that's true.
For in the briefest embrace of time,
We glimpse forever breaking through.

The Connection of Kindred Spirits

Through tangled paths, we wander free,
With hearts aligned, we find our way.
Each smile shared, a sacred bond,
In echoes of the words we say.

Between the lines of stories told,
Our souls entwine, a softer glow.
In laughter shared, in silence felt,
The kindred spirits ebb and flow.

No distance vast can break the ties,
That pull us close, like stars that sing.
For in each heartbeat, there resides,
The love that only we can bring.

Together woven in the night,
A fabric bright, where dreams take flight.
In every moment, near or far,
Our spirits dance, a guiding star.

The Embrace of the Untold

In shadows lie the stories deep,
Yet whispered winds can tell their tales.
The unknown calls, a beckoning,
Inviting dreams where wonder sails.

Beyond the edge of sight and sound,
The truths await, untouched, unclaimed.
In silence, mysteries unfold,
As hearts ignite, unbound, untamed.

Between the words, a yearning breath,
To find the paths of souls once lost.
The embrace of every secret held,
Awaits to share its quiet cost.

For in the fold of time's embrace,
Lies magic wrapped in hope's soft glow.
Let courage guide you through the dark,
To find the light of what we know.

Echoes in the Enchanted Forest

Whispers dance upon the breeze,
Ancient trees sway with ease.
Moonlight spills on mossy ground,
Magic lingers all around.

Shadows wander, secrets old,
Stories waiting to be told.
Creaking branches, nature's song,
In this realm, we all belong.

Footsteps fade, yet spirits roam,
In the woods, we find our home.
Echoes of forgotten dreams,
In the night, the forest gleams.

The Light in the Labyrinth

Winding paths twist and twine,
Lost in thoughts, our fears entwine.
Flickers glow, a guiding spark,
Through the shadows, find the mark.

Around each bend, a choice awaits,
Dreams and doubts, they hesitate.
Yet in the heart, a flame so bright,
Illuminates the darkest night.

Trust the journey, step with grace,
Every turn reveals a face.
Together we'll forge our way free,
In this maze, you walk with me.

The Heartbeat of Stillness

In the quiet, a pulse so deep,
Whispers of the world asleep.
Time stands still, a gentle sigh,
In this moment, we comply.

Softly breathing, hearts align,
In the hush, our spirits shine.
Nature's rhythm, calm and pure,
In stillness, we find our cure.

Eyes closed tight, we sense the whole,
In silence, we touch the soul.
Every heartbeat echoes clear,
In stillness, we have no fear.

The Language of the Unheard

Words unspoken, voices shy,
In their silence, dreams still fly.
Hidden messages in the air,
Listening closely, hearts laid bare.

Thoughts entwined in gentle grace,
Finding truth in every place.
In the quiet, wisdom swells,
Where the heart's soft story dwells.

Eyes that speak, a knowing glance,
In their gaze, we find our chance.
Together we'll understand the art,
Of the language that fills the heart.

Shades of Delicate Mystery

In twilight's soft and tender glow,
Whispers dance as shadows flow,
Colors blend in secret sighs,
Beneath the veil, the silence lies.

Amidst the leaves, a story weaves,
Soft echoes linger, the heart believes,
In every glance, a tale untold,
Fragrant dreams in hues of gold.

The moonlight plays on silver streams,
As night unfolds its quiet dreams,
A gentle breeze stirs memories' flight,
Cradling hope in the still of night.

Each moment, wrapped in mystery's lace,
Hides a world, a secret place,
Where thoughts and whispers intertwine,
And life surrenders to the divine.

The Fabric of Time's Embrace

Threads of moments weave so fine,
Capturing glimpses, the heart's design,
Each tick a note in the song of days,
As we wander through time's gentle haze.

A tapestry bright with joy and pain,
Woven paths that leave a stain,
In every choice, the threads pull tight,
Fading fast into the night.

Hours unfold in serene delight,
A fusion of shadow and light,
In the silence, stories hum,
While history's soft echoes drum.

Time's embrace, a warm cocoon,
Cradling dreams beneath the moon,
As we measure what is sore,
In the fabric, we find our core.

Gentle Chimes of Possibility

Beneath the arch of a softly ringing bell,
Whispers float where dreams do dwell,
Each chime a wish, a spark of hope,
Guiding hearts along a tightrope.

In quiet corners of the mind,
New paths emerge, the soul aligned,
A gentle nudge from fate's own hand,
Inviting us to understand.

The wind carries secrets, soft and sweet,
A dance of chances beneath our feet,
With every note, a door swings wide,
Awakening wonders that reside inside.

As dreams collide with waking hours,
We bloom like stars, we break like flowers,
With gentle chimes, the world awakes,
To possibilities that life remakes.

The Symphony of the Unperceived

In silence blooms a world unseen,
A symphony of what has been,
The rustling leaves, the breath of air,
Compose a melody, everywhere.

Under the surface, the heartbeat flows,
In shadowed realms, the mystery grows,
Each silent note, a story waits,
As time reveals the hidden fates.

Awakening senses, the whispers rise,
In colors soft, the heart complies,
A tumult of feelings, pure and unkempt,
In the hush, emotions are exempt.

The unperceived sings a haunting tune,
A dance of shadows beneath the moon,
Connecting us all in the still of night,
Where the unseen world takes flight.

Veils of Silk and Stardust

Veils of silk, a whisper soft,
Glimmers dance, as dreams take off.
Underneath a midnight sky,
Stardust falls, and hopes can fly.

Threads of silver, gold entwined,
In the shadows, treasures find.
Glistening paths where wishes glide,
In every fold, a secret hides.

Crimson petals, fragrant schemes,
Wrapped in longing, woven dreams.
Velvet nights and morning's light,
Weaving tales from dark to bright.

Looms of fate, the fabric spun,
Embrace the dawn, a new day begun.
In stillness, a soft heart's hymn,
Veils of silk, and stars grow dim.

Soft Murmurs Beneath the Surface

In the quiet, whispers flow,
Soft murmurs where the shadows grow.
Beneath the waves, secrets sigh,
Echoes of the night sky high.

Gentle ripples, hearts collide,
In the stillness, dreams abide.
Underneath the surface bare,
Voices rise like tender air.

Hidden currents, pull and sway,
Guiding thoughts that drift away.
In the depths, our wishes hide,
Soft murmurs, the soul's own tide.

As the currents weave and curl,
We find peace within this world.
Softly spoken, love's embrace,
Beneath the surface, find your place.

The Language of Lost Things

In a pocket of dreams untold,
Lie the remnants, soft and old.
Whispers of a time long past,
In the silence, shadows cast.

Forgotten words on paper's edge,
Echo softly, a solemn pledge.
The language formed in whispered song,
Where the lost and found belong.

In the corners of the mind,
Faded treasures, yet to find.
Echoes of a silent ring,
Speak to us, the lost things sing.

Through the corridors of yore,
Every memory, an open door.
In the tapestry of space and time,
Languages lost, yet still they rhyme.

Hidden Harmonies of the Heart

In the stillness, hearts entwined,
Hidden melodies we find.
Softest notes, a secret call,
In whispered dreams, we rise and fall.

Each heartbeat, a gentle chord,
In the silence, love adored.
Dances move on fragile air,
Harmony lives, woven with care.

Underneath the moonlit hue,
Soundless whispers, pure and true.
In the depths, where feelings lay,
Hidden harmonies softly play.

In every glance, a rhythm flows,
In every touch, the music grows.
Together we create our art,
In hidden harmonies of the heart.

Secrets of the Unseen

In shadows deep where silence sighs,
Mysteries dance, hidden from eyes.
Whispers flutter, soft as a breeze,
Unraveling truths among the trees.

The night conceals what daylight reveals,
Ancient tales the darkness steals.
Gentle secrets held in the night,
Call to the heart, igniting the light.

Echoes in the Twilight

As day gives way to evening's glow,
Faint echoes rise, soft and low.
Images linger, flicker, and fade,
Tales of the past in dusk's serenade.

Veils of time weave through the air,
Lost moments sigh, a gentle prayer.
Whispers dance in the waning light,
In twilight's hush, everything feels right.

Threads of Enchantment

In the fabric of dreams, a pattern unfolds,
Threads of enchantment, stories untold.
Stitched with starlight, woven with care,
A tapestry rich with magic to share.

Colors entwine, vivid and bright,
Each strand a wish, a spark of delight.
In this realm where wonder beams,
We find our paths within our dreams.

Murmurs of the Mystical

In quiet corners where shadows reside,
Murmurs of magic, the soul's gentle guide.
Laughter and sorrow, both intertwined,
A tapestry thick with the tales of mankind.

Under the moon's watchful gaze,
Wisdom unfolds in myriad ways.
The mystical beats in the heart's quiet song,
A melody born where we all belong.

The Allure of the Unspoken

In quiet corners where whispers dwell,
Secrets linger, casting a spell.
Words left unsaid tightly entwine,
A dance of silence, a truth divine.

Eyes meet shyly, stories unfold,
In hues of silence, emotions bold.
The heart speaks softly, a gentle tune,
In the allure of night, beneath the moon.

Each glance, a chapter, unturned, unread,
The language of feelings, quietly spread.
Mysteries hidden in the softest sigh,
The beauty of silence, no need to try.

In the pause between breaths, we find,
An unspoken bond that ties the mind.
In moments of quiet, so much to claim,
In the allure of the unspoken, the same.

An Overture of Shadows

Beneath the twilight, shadows creep,
Whispers echo, secrets to keep.
An overture sung in the night's embrace,
The dance of darkness, a soft trace.

Figures flicker in the dim-lit glow,
Stories unravel where few dare go.
The silence hums with tales untold,
In the grip of night, the heart grows bold.

Each murmur stirs the restless air,
A melody haunting, soft as a prayer.
In the realm of shadows, we gaze and sigh,
Beneath the velvet, the night's lullaby.

An overture of shadows whispers low,
In the absence of light, our dreams will flow.
With every heartbeat, the night will sing,
In the dance of darkness, we take wing.

Songs of the Unimagined

In realms where thoughts take flight and soar,
Melodies rise, forevermore.
Songs of the unimagined, wild and free,
An echo of dreams, a symphony.

From colors unseen, harmonies bloom,
In spaces of silence, dispelling the gloom.
Voices entwine with the threads of time,
Creating a tapestry, bright and sublime.

The heart beats softly, in rhythm divine,
In worlds uncharted, where hopes intertwine.
Each note a whisper, a spark in the dark,
Illuminating paths, igniting a spark.

Songs of the unimagined softly play,
Guiding lost souls along the way.
In echoes of wonder, we find our truth,
In the music of dreams, we reclaim our youth.

The Pulse of Paradox

In the heartbeat of chaos, calm resides,
Where questions linger and wonder hides.
The pulse of paradox beats strong and true,
In duality's dance, we find something new.

Light and shadow, entwined in a fight,
Crafting the fabric of day and night.
In contradictions, we seek to understand,
The beauty in balance, a delicate hand.

Life's complexities weave tales of grace,
In every challenge, we find our place.
The pulse of paradox flows through our veins,
In every storm, a quiet remains.

Embrace the enigma, let it unfold,
For in every story, a truth to be told.
In the pulse of paradox, hearts shall align,
In life's rich tapestry, we find the divine.

Lullabies of the Night Sky

Stars whisper softly, a gentle embrace,
Moonlight cascades, painting dreams in grace.
Clouds drift like wishes on a silken thread,
The world finds solace in the words unsaid.

Crickets sing lullabies, sweet and low,
Night wraps its arms, letting the stillness grow.
Each heartbeat echoes a tranquil refrain,
As the sky cradles hope, like a soothing rain.

Sleep blooms like petals, under twilight's glow,
Embracing the silence, letting worries go.
In the arms of the night, peace takes its flight,
Wrapped in the beauty of dreams catching light.

With every twinkle, a story is spun,
The night breathes softly, inviting the fun.
Whispers of starlight guide us away,
Into the magic where shadows play.

Silhouettes of Serendipity

In twilight's embrace, shadows stretch long,
Unexpected moments hum a sweet song.
Paths converge lightly, like whispers in air,
Creating a tapestry of fated prayer.

Each turn reveals more than the eyes can see,
Serendipity dances, wild and free.
The heart feels its flutter, the soul takes a chance,
In the shadows of fate, we all learn to dance.

Gentle are the footsteps that lead us to light,
Unexpected friends found in the night.
A smile shared softly, a glance that ignites,
Time weaves its magic, like fireflies' flights.

The canvas of life is splashed with delight,
As silhouettes mingle and chase the night.
Every heartbeat a story, every glance a song,
In the embrace of the shadows, we all belong.

Chasing Fleeting Fantasies

Dreams drift like whispers on a summer's breeze,
Elusive are visions that dance through the trees.
Each thought like a feather, light as the dawn,
Chasing the shadows, where hopes are reborn.

Moments slip past like grains in the sand,
Fleeting illusions, we try to command.
A flicker of magic in the corner of dreams,
Reality ripples, unraveling seams.

In laughter and yearning, we search high and low,
For the fleeting moments that shimmer and glow.
With eyes wide open, we dare to explore,
The landscapes of wonder that beckon us more.

Letting go gently, we dance with the breeze,
Chasing the fleeting, embracing heart's keys.
For in every flash, there's a story we find,
A treasure of dreams entwined in the mind.

Tapestry of the Unknown

Woven from whispers of tales never told,
The unknown stretches, both timid and bold.
Threads of adventure interlace our way,
Crafting a future where shadows can play.

Colors collide in a dance of delight,
Curiosity flickers, igniting the night.
Questions unravel, inviting the guess,
The tapestry tells of both chaos and mess.

Boundless horizons where dreams come alive,
In the heart of the unknown, our spirits thrive.
With every step taken, new stories unfold,
A journey to cherish, a treasure to hold.

Let courage be woven with fibers of hope,
As we navigate pathways, learning to cope.
In the tapestry's threads, let us find our song,
Embracing the unknown, where we all belong.

Milton Keynes UK
Ingram Content Group UK Ltd.
UKHW020816141124
451205UK00012B/613

9 789916 905456